cooking the
Italian way

Pasta Cinese makes a filling and delicious main dish. (Recipe on page 28.)

cooking the
Italian way

ALPHONSE BISIGNANO

easy menu
ethnic
cookbooks

Lerner Publications Company ▪ Minneapolis

Series Editor: Patricia A. Grotts
Series Consultant: Ann L. Burckhardt

Drawings and Map by Jeanette Swofford
Photographs by Robert L. and Diane Wolfe

Additional photographs are reproduced through the courtesy of Alitalia Airlines (pp. 9, 11, 16) and the National Live Stock & Meat Board (p. 39).

Library of Congress Cataloging in Publication Data

Bisignano, Alphonse.
  Cooking the Italian way.

  (Easy menu ethnic cookbooks)
  Includes index.
  Summary: Introduces the land, people, and regional cooking of Italy and includes recipes for such dishes as minestrone soup, spaghetti with meat sauce, and chicken cacciatore.
    1. Cookery, Italian—Juvenile literature. 2. Italy—Juvenile literature. [1. Cookery, Italian] I. Wolfe, Robert L., ill. II. Swofford, Jeanette, ill. III. Title. IV. Series.
TX723.B49 1982   641.5945   82-12641
ISBN 0-8225-0906-7 (lib. bdg.)

Manufactured in the United States of America

  4 5 6 7 8 9 10 88 87 86 85

Minestrone **is a perfect hot soup to serve on a cool day. (Recipe on page 24.)**

CONTENTS

Sausage

Dairy Products

Grain

Alps
Piedmont •Milan Alps
Turin• Po River Po River
Venice
Liguria •Genoa Emilia-Romagna
Bologna

Seafood

Seafood Grapes
Wine

Arno River
Florence Adriatic Sea
Tuscany
Sienna
Ligurian Sea

Ice Cream

ITALY
•Rome Vegetables

Flag of Italy

Goats Grapes Naples• Bari•
Sardinia
Wine
Sheep Olive Oil
Tyrrhenian Sea Calabria
Pasta Olives

Goats Citrus Fruit
Hogs
Palermo•
Mediterranean Sea •Catania
Sicily Ionian Sea
Olives

Apennine Mountains

Tiber River

INTRODUCTION

The words "Italian cooking" make many people think of pizza, ravioli, and spaghetti smothered in tomato sauce. Juicy tomatoes, cheese, and tasty noodles are ingredients often used by Italian cooks, but other foods are just as important. As the recipes in this book show, sausages, olives, rice, and colorful fruits and vegetables make the cooking of Italy as varied as it is delicious.

THE LAND AND ITS PEOPLE

Italy is a boot-shaped peninsula that extends into the Mediterranean Sea. (The large islands of Sicily and Sardinia are also part of Italy.) The majestic Alps link Italy to the rest of Europe, and the Apennine mountain range runs from the Tuscany region down to the peninsula's southern tip. Many valleys are located in these mountains, and before modern transportation methods, the people who lived in them were very isolated. The lack of communication between the Italian people made Italy a divided nation for a long time.

Because the people of each region were loyal to their own area rather than to Italy as a whole, it was easy for other more powerful nations to take control of the Italian government. Italy passed through periods of Spanish, Austrian, and French rule before becoming an independent country. Not until 1861 did the Italian people become united under one ruler, Victor Emmanuel II.

Even after this unification, however, regional differences remained. The people of each region had developed their own ways of doing things—especially in the kitchen. They were very proud of their distinctive cooking styles and passed down recipes from generation to generation.

REGIONAL COOKING

Northern and southern Italy are different from one another. Whereas the north has very fertile land and a large, wealthy population, the south has dry land and a smaller, poorer population. The difference in climate affects the ingredients available for cooking, and this makes the dishes of northern and southern Italy distinct. Each of Italy's 20 regions has its own specialties, too.

The northwestern region of Piedmont is known for its fragrant and sparkling wines, and its chief agricultural product is rice. In fact, it is the greatest rice-producing area in Italy, and Italy is Europe's biggest producer of rice. The northeastern regions and the city of Venice are also known for their rice dishes and for their fish dishes. Delicacies such as sole, anchovies, mackerel, eel, spiny lobster, shrimp, scampi, and squid from the Adriatic Sea are cooked simply so that their fresh flavor comes through.

The region of Liguria uses seafood in its cooking, too, but it is best known for the use of fragrant herbs. Rosemary, basil, sage, marjoram, and others all decorate Liguria's hillsides. These herbs add special flavors to the dishes of this area.

Perhaps the richest cooking is found in the fertile region of Emilia-Romagna, where butter is the main cooking fat. Emilia-Romagna's specialties include homemade pasta (Emilia-Romagna is Italy's largest producer of wheat), vegetables, fruit, hams, sausages, and rich dairy products, including

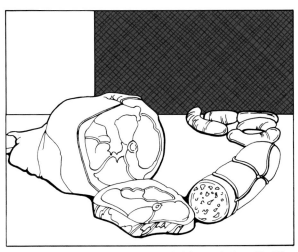

Ham and sausage are specialties of the Emilia-Romagna region.

Parmesan cheese. Bologna, the chief city of that region, is known as "la grassa" (the fat one). It specializes in delicious goose sausages and green lasagna. (For green lasagna, spinach is added to the pasta dough.) Bologna's most famous pork product is *mortadella* (mort-ah-DAYL-lah)—a smoothly textured, delicately flavored sausage that can be as large as 18 inches around!

South of Emilia-Romagna is the region of Tuscany, whose capital is Florence. This region is known for its use of high-quality ingredients and a minimum of sauces and seasonings. It is simple home cooking at its best.

Italian cooking changes once again south of the Tuscany region. The Apennine Mountains and foothills spread from coast to coast, and olive trees growing on the hillside replace the fat dairy cows of the north. Olive oil is the dominant cooking fat, and economical, mass-produced, hard macaroni takes the place of soft, homemade pasta.

Grapes for wine are grown throughout Italy. The vineyard shown here is near Rome.

The city of Naples is known for its pizza made with thick red tomato sauce and creamy mozzarella cheese. Further south, as the climate becomes warmer, vegetables have bright, vibrant colors, and pastas are so strongly flavored that a topping is often not needed. Heavy, rich sweets are also enjoyed in the south, particularly in Sicily. This island's volcanic soil is excellent for growing citrus fruits, olives, and grapes.

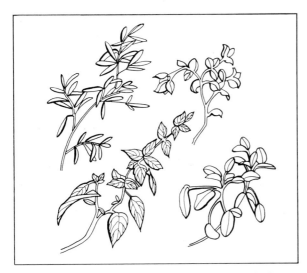

Herbs often used in Italian cooking include rosemary, marjoram, basil, and sage.

AN ITALIAN MARKET

Fine, fresh vegetables are found throughout Italy. In each city or town, outdoor markets are usually located near the main piazza or cathedral. The vegetable stalls found on dusty side streets are ablaze with the colors of Italy's finest produce—red tomatoes, green zucchini, purple eggplant, and bright orange carrots are artistically displayed.

In the spring and fall, fresh wild mushrooms take their place alongside the vegetables: brown, orange, and cream-colored varieties can all be found, and Italians find each a special seasonal treat.

Hanging above the produce, festoons of dried and fresh herbs wave in the breeze. Bunches of parsley, basil, marjoram, thyme, rosemary, and more are bought at the market and brought home to become an indispensable part of the Italian kitchen. Also hanging from market stalls are abundant poultry and game. Ducks, geese, chickens, and turkeys are ready for each shopper's inspection, and, in some areas, there are deer and wild boar as well.

After a morning of shopping in the market, both young and old find the local ice cream vendor a welcome sight. Italy has perhaps the best ice cream in the world: *gelati* (jay-LAH-tee) is a milk-based ice cream that is much like the chocolate and vanilla ice cream found in North America, and *granita* (grah-NEE-tah) is a light sherbet made of ice and syrup. Popular flavors include coffee, lemon, and strawberry. Each is sure to disappear deliciously the second it touches the tongue!

To finish their shopping, Italian cooks may stop at a pastry shop, or *pasticceria* (pah-steech-eh-REE-yah). There they will buy pastries to be eaten in midmorning or mid-afternoon rather than after a meal. More elaborate sweets are reserved for special occasions, and each region of Italy has its own favorite. Rome, for example, relishes a smooth ricotta cheese pie; southern Italy enjoys chewy macaroons, and the city of Milan is famous for its *panettone* (pahn-ayt-TOH-nay), a tall, light yellow cake studded with raisins and candied fruit. It is eaten at Christmastime and at Easter in particular, and it is even exported to the United States.

A wide variety of goods, including fresh fruits and vegetables, ice cream and other sweets, and flowers (above), can be purchased from Italian street vendors.

BEFORE YOU BEGIN

Cooking any dish, plain or fancy, is easier and more fun if you are familiar with the ingredients. Italian cooking makes use of some ingredients that you may not know. Sometimes special cookware is used, too, although the recipes in this book can easily be prepared with ordinary utensils and pans.

Before you start cooking, carefully study the following "dictionary" of terms and special ingredients. Then read through the recipe you want to try from beginning to end. Now you are ready to shop for ingredients and to organize the cookware you will need. Once you have assembled everything, you can begin to cook. Before you start, it is also very important to read *The Careful Cook* on page 43. Following these rules will make your cooking experience safe, fun, and easy.

A colander and a Dutch oven (front) are utensils often used by Italian cooks.

COOKING UTENSILS

colander — A bowl-shaped dish with holes in it that is used for washing or draining food

Dutch oven — A heavy pot with a tight-fitting domed cover that is often used for cooking soups or stews

COOKING TERMS

al dente — An Italian cooking term, literally meaning "to the tooth," that describes the point at which pasta is properly cooked — firm and tender to bite, but not soft

boil — To heat a liquid over high heat until bubbles form and rise rapidly to the surface

brown — To cook food quickly in fat over high heat so that the surface turns an even brown

dice — To chop food into small, square-shaped pieces

fold — To blend an ingredient with other ingredients by using a gentle overturning circular motion instead of by stirring or beating

grate — To cut into tiny pieces by rubbing the food against a grater; to shred

hard-cook — To cook an egg in its shell until both the yolk and white are firm

mince — To chop food into very small pieces

preheat — To allow an oven to warm up to a certain temperature before putting food in it

sauté — To fry quickly over high heat in oil or fat, stirring or turning the food to prevent burning

shred — To tear or cut into small pieces, either by hand or with a grater

simmer — To cook over low heat in liquid kept just below its boiling point. Bubbles may occasionally rise to the surface.

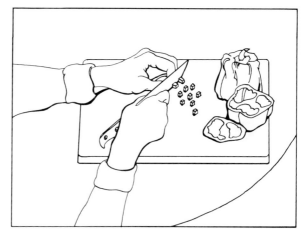

To dice a green pepper, first slice it crosswise into rings. Then cut each ring into small, square-shaped pieces.

SPECIAL INGREDIENTS

almond extract — A liquid made from the oil of the almond nut and used to give an almond flavor to food

artichoke — An herb with a green, thistle-like head that is eaten as a vegetable. The tender center of the artichoke, called the *heart*, has a delicate flavor and is often used in salads. Canned artichoke hearts are packed in either water or oil and vinegar.

basil — A rich and fragrant herb whose dried leaves are used in cooking

bay leaf — The dried leaf of the bay (also called laurel) tree. It is used to season food.

cheeses

   mozzarella — A moist, white, unsalted cheese with a mild flavor and a smooth rubbery texture

   Parmesan — A hard, dry, sharply flavored Italian cheese

   pimento cheese — A cheese to which chopped pimento has been added

   provolone — A creamy, yellow Italian cheese with a mild, buttery flavor

   ricotta — A soft, creamy, unsalted Italian cheese that is similar in texture to cream cheese but more like cottage cheese in flavor

   Romano — A hard Italian cheese with a sharper flavor than Parmesan

dry mustard — A powder made from the ground seeds of the mustard plant that is used to flavor food

garlic — An herb whose distinctive flavor is used in many dishes. Fresh garlic can usually be found in the produce department of a supermarket. Each piece or *bulb* can be broken up into several small sections called cloves. Most recipes use only one or two finely chopped cloves of this very strong herb. Before you chop up a clove of garlic, you will have to remove the brittle, papery covering that surrounds it.

Italian sausage — A sausage made from ground pork, seasonings, and preservatives and packed into an edible casing

kidney bean — A large kidney-shaped red bean

maraschino cherries — Large cherries preserved in a sweet liquid

nutmeg — A fragrant spice, either whole or ground, that is often used in desserts

olive oil — An oil made from pressed olives that is used in cooking and for dressing salads

oregano — The dried leaves, whole or powdered, of a rich and fragrant herb that is used as a seasoning in cooking

paprika — A red seasoning made from ground, dried pods of the *capsicum* pepper plant. It has a sweeter flavor than red pepper.

pasta

    elbow macaroni — Smooth, curved, tube-shaped noodles about 1 inch long

    fettucini — Noodles in the form of narrow ribbons

    mostaccioli — Ridged, tube-shaped noodles about 2 inches long

    rigatoni — Short, slightly curved, fluted noodles

spaghetti — Noodles made in the form of long, thin strands

spinach noodles — Noodles made with spinach that are green in color

prosciutto — Dry, cured ham that is pale red in color and has a delicate, sweet flavor

scallions — Another name for green onions

white wine vinegar — A vinegar made with white wine

yeast — An ingredient used in baking that causes dough to rise up and become light and fluffy. Yeast is available in either small, white cakes called compressed yeast or in granular form called active dry yeast.

Many Italian restaurants have sidewalk tables so customers can sit outside in nice weather.

AN ITALIAN TABLE

An Italian dining table is generally covered with a fine linen tablecloth. A bowl of fresh fruit provides color, as does the bottle of wine that is usually present at every meal except breakfast. Diners help themselves to slices from the large hunks of cheese, rolls of sausage, and loaves of bread (always served without butter) that are often placed on the table.

A small glass filled with toothpicks is another familiar sight on an Italian table. The Italian word for toothpicks is *stuzzicadenti* (stoot-zee-cah-DEN-tee), but the Italians have labeled them *l'ultimo piattanzo* (L'OOL-tee-moh pee-aht-TAHN-zoh), or "the last course."

The Italian table is set with all of the silver and glasses to be used during the meal. Each diner sits before a flat plate with a soup plate placed on top of it. The soup or pasta is served into the top dish, which is then removed for the following courses. Italians always eat their meals in stages—one course at a time.

In the Italian home, eating is a leisurely affair. Family members of all ages gather around the table to enjoy a delicious meal. Italian cooks take pride in presenting their finest dishes to their families and close friends. When you learn how to make the recipes in this book, you can do the same.

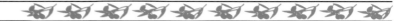

AN ITALIAN MENU

Below is a simplified menu plan for a typical day of Italian cooking. The Italian names of the dishes are given, along with a guide on how to pronounce them. Two alternate dinner ideas are included. Recipes for the starred items can be found in this book.

ENGLISH	ITALIANO	PRONUNCIATION GUIDE
MENU	LA LISTA	lah LEE-stah
Breakfast	*La Prima Colazione*	lah PREE-mah co-lah-tzee-YOH-nay
Coffee	Caffè	kah-FAY
Pastry	Pasticceria	pah-steech-eh-REE-yah
Dinner	*Il Pranzo*	eel PRAHN-zoh
I	I	
*Appetizer	Antipasto	ahn-tee-PAH-stoh
*Italian salad dressing	Condimento Italiano	kohn-dee-MAYN-toh ee-tahl-YAH-noh
	per insalata	pehr een-sah-LAH-tah
*Chinese pasta or	Pasta Cinese o	PAH-stah chin-AY-zay oh
*Straw and hay	Paglia e fieno	PAHL-yah ay FYAY-noh
*Italian-style pork chops	Costolette di	kohs-toh-LET-tay dee
	maiale Italiano	may-YAH-leh ee-tahl-YAH-noh
*Bisignano spinach	Spinaci Bisignano	speen-AH-chee bee-zee-NYAH-noh
Fresh fruit	Frutta fresca	FROOT-tah FRES-kah

ENGLISH	ITALIANO	PRONUNCIATION GUIDE
II	**II**	
*Minestrone	Minestrone	mee-neh-STROH-nay
*Spaghetti with meat sauce or	Spaghetti al sugo o	spah-GET-tee ahl SOO-goh oh
*Risotto	Risotto	ree-ZOHT-oh
*Chicken hunter's style	Pollo alla cacciatore	POH-loh AH-lah kah-chah-TOH-ray
*Italian-style cauliflower	Cavolfiore Italiano	kah-vohl-FYOH-ray ee-tahl-YAH-noh
Fresh fruit	Frutta fresca	FROOT-tah FRES-kah
Supper	***La Cena***	lah CHAY-nah
*Pizza	Pizza	PEE-tsah
Green salad	Insalata verde	een-sah-LAH-tah VEHR-day
*Biscuit tortoni	Tortoni	tor-TOH-nee

rosemary

basil

marjoram

sage

BREAKFAST/
La Prima Colazione

Although many Italians have a hearty diet, they often start out their day with a rather small meal. A typical breakfast may consist of only a cup of coffee with milk and maybe a pastry.

DINNER/
Il Pranzo

By 12:00 P.M., most Italians who have breakfasted lightly are ready for a big dinner with several courses. There is no main course in an Italian meal. Instead, there are at least two principal courses that are never brought to the table at the same time. The meal usually starts with the *antipasto*, or appetizer. The purpose of this plate is to get the diner's stomach ready for the soup, which is followed by the pasta. After the pasta, the course of meat or fish is served, along with side dishes of cooked vegetables. The vegetables often reflect the colors of the season. Early peas and asparagus are found on a table in springtime; cauliflower and artichokes are winter fare, and bright tomatoes, eggplant, and green pepper liven up summer meals.

Italians generally drink wine with their meals. (Even the children in Italy drink wine, although it is diluted with water or soda pop.) Dessert in Italy is usually a piece of fruit, which is always cut into small pieces before

Colorful *antipasto* looks as good as it tastes. (Recipe on page 22.)

it is eaten. It "clears the palate" and cleans the teeth. After the meal, Italians may enjoy a strong black coffee called *espresso*. Coffee time, however, is generally at about 4:00 P.M. At that time, cups of either *espresso* or *cappuccino* (kah-poo-CHEE-noh) are served. *Cappuccino* is *espresso* with a layer of steamed milk on top.

Espresso **is often served in a tiny cup and saucer.**

Appetizer/
Antipasto

Antipasto is an Italian word that comes from Latin. Ante *means "before" and* pasto *means "pasta" or dough. Antipasto is, therefore, what you eat before the pasta.*

  several leaves of leaf lettuce
½ **head fresh greens, such as Boston or romaine lettuce, shredded**
6 **carrots, peeled, halved, and cut into 3-inch pieces**
6 **celery stalks, cut into 3-inch pieces**
6 **salami slices**
6 **provolone or mozzarella cheese slices**
2 **tomatoes**
2 **hard-cooked eggs**
6 **canned artichoke hearts, packed in oil and vinegar**
  black and green olives for garnish
  radishes for garnish
  bunch of scallions for garnish
¼ **cup Italian salad dressing (recipe follows)**

1. Wash all fresh vegetables thoroughly and let dry.
2. Cover a large serving plate with leaf lettuce. Place shredded greens on top.
3. Divide carrot and celery sticks in half and place at each end of the plate.
4. In the center of the plate, lay alternate slices of salami and cheese.
5. Cut tomatoes and hard-cooked eggs into quarters. Arrange egg and tomato quarters and artichoke hearts around the edge of the plate.
6. Place olives, a few radishes, and some scallions wherever they fit in attractively. (Any other fresh raw vegetables such as broccoli or cauliflower cut into bite-sized pieces may be added.)
7. Dribble salad dressing over all.

Serves 6 to 8

Italian Salad Dressing/
Condimento Italiano per Insalata

1 cup olive oil
¼ cup white wine vinegar
2 tablespoons lemon juice
1 teaspoon salt
½ teaspoon pepper
1 teaspoon sugar
½ teaspoon dry mustard
¼ teaspoon paprika
½ teaspoon oregano
⅛ teaspoon basil
1 clove garlic, crushed

1. Combine all ingredients in a tightly covered jar. Shake well until dressing is thoroughly mixed.
2. Refrigerate for 2 hours. Shake well before serving.

Makes 1½ cups

Minestrone

Minestrone *is a rich, thick vegetable soup that almost makes a meal in itself. It gets its name from the Latin word* minestrare, *which means "to serve" or "dish up."*

1 16-ounce can (2 cups) kidney
   beans
1 clove garlic, minced
½ teaspoon salt
¼ teaspoon pepper
1 tablespoon vegetable oil
¼ cup chopped fresh parsley
1 small fresh zucchini, unpeeled and
   diced
2 celery stalks with leaves, finely
   chopped
2 small carrots, peeled and diced
1 small onion, minced
1 16-ounce can (2 cups) whole
   tomatoes, cut up with a spoon
3 tablespoons butter or margarine
2½ cups water
⅓ cup elbow macaroni, uncooked
½ cup beef bouillon or tomato juice
   salt to taste

1. Put beans in a large kettle and mash them slightly with a fork.
2. Add garlic, salt, pepper, oil, and parsley. Stir well.
3. Add all vegetables, butter, and water to the kettle. Bring to a boil over medium heat, stirring occasionally.
4. Lower heat, cover the kettle, and simmer 1 hour, stirring occasionally.
5. After 1 hour, add macaroni and beef bouillon or tomato juice. Simmer 15 minutes, stirring occasionally. Add salt to taste.

Serves 6 to 8

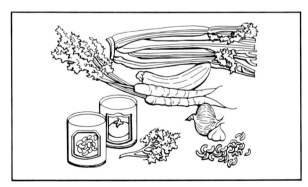

Ingredients used in *minestrone* include celery, zucchini, carrots, kidney beans, tomatoes, parsley, garlic, and elbow macaroni.

Risotto

Risotto *is a creamy delicacy made with white rice. If you like to stir, you'll like preparing this dish.*

2 to 2½ 15-ounce cans (about 4 to 5 cups) chicken broth
4 tablespoons butter
2 tablespoons vegetable oil
2 tablespoons minced onion
1½ cups white rice, uncooked
⅔ cup grated Parmesan cheese

1. Heat broth until simmering.
2. In a heavy saucepan, heat 2 table-spoons butter with the oil. Sauté onion in butter and oil until golden.
3. Add rice and stir until well coated. Sauté rice briefly, then add ½ cup of the simmering broth. Cook over medium heat, stirring constantly, until rice absorbs liquid. Then add another ½ cup broth. Continue cooking and stirring, adding another ½ cup broth each time rice dries out. (This will take about 30 minutes.

When finished, rice will be creamy and tender, yet firm.)
4. When rice is almost done, add grated cheese and remaining 2 tablespoons butter. If needed, season with a little salt. Serve immediately. Pass more grated Parmesan cheese at the table.

Serves 6

Rice, Parmesan cheese, and onion are the main ingredients of *risotto*.

Paglia e fieno is a tasty pasta dish, rich with cream and Parmesan cheese.

Straw and Hay/
Paglia e Fieno

These creamy noodles originated in the city of Sienna, which still has the look of the Middle Ages. The green noodles are the "hay," and the white noodles are the "straw."

For a tasty variation, sauté 1 cup thinly sliced cooked ham with the peas and mushrooms and serve the finished dish as a main course.

4 ounces (¼ pound) thin spinach noodles, uncooked
4 ounces (¼ pound) fettucini noodles, uncooked
3 tablespoons butter
1 clove garlic, minced
4 ounces (½ cup) tiny canned peas, drained (optional)
¼ pound fresh mushrooms, sliced
¾ cup whipping cream
½ teaspoon salt
pepper to taste
¼ cup grated Parmesan cheese

1. Cook noodles in boiling salted water until they are *al dente*. Drain and toss with 1½ tablespoons butter. Cover and set aside.
2. Melt remaining 1½ tablespoons butter in a large saucepan. Sauté garlic until golden. Spoon out garlic and discard.
3. In the same butter, sauté peas and mushrooms over low heat for 5 minutes. At the same time, heat cream in a small pan. (Do not boil.)
4. Add noodles, cream, salt, and pepper to vegetables in the large saucepan. With the pan still over heat, toss vigorously with a long-handled spoon and fork.
5. Remove from heat and quickly stir in cheese. Serve on warm plates. Pass more grated Parmesan cheese at the table.

Serves 4

Chinese Pasta/
Pasta Cinese

In spite of its Oriental name, this pasta is very Italian. As with any pasta dish, this one is quite filling and can be eaten as a meal in itself. For Pasta Cinese, *you will make a sauce and meatballs that can be used in other dishes or served alone as a side dish.*

Sauce ingredients:

1 **12-ounce can (about 1½ cups) tomato paste**
3 **cups water**
1 **teaspoon basil**
1 **teaspoon oregano**
1 **large bay leaf**
1 **clove garlic, minced**
1 **medium-sized onion, chopped**
1 **tablespoon salt**
  dash of pepper
2 **or 3 Italian sausage links (optional)**

1. Combine all ingredients in a Dutch oven. Cover and simmer over low heat for 2 hours, stirring occasionally.* (If sauce becomes too thick and begins to stick to the sides of the oven, add a little water.)
2. Remove the lid about 15 minutes before serving so that sauce can thicken. (Sauce should be heavy and smooth.)
Makes 1 quart of sauce

*While the sauce is simmering for 2 hours, you will have plenty of time to prepare the rest of the dish.

Meatball ingredients:

½ **pound lean ground beef**
½ **cup cracker or bread crumbs**
1 **egg**
  pinch of oregano
  pinch of basil
  salt to taste
  pepper to taste
1 **clove garlic, minced**
1 **small onion, finely chopped**
2 **tablespoons grated Romano or Parmesan cheese**
  vegetable oil for frying

1. Put all ingredients except oil in a large bowl and mix well. (Many cooks use their hands for mixing meatballs.)

2. Roll about 1 tablespoon meat between the palms of your hands to make meatballs that are ¾ inch in diameter.

3. In a frying pan, brown meatballs in about ½ inch of oil and drain. (Or, place meatballs in a shallow pan and bake at 350° for about 10 minutes.)

Makes 25 to 30 small meatballs

Pasta ingredients:

**8 ounces (½ pound) mostaccioli or
    rigatoni noodles, uncooked
1 quart sauce
25 to 30 small meatballs
 1 or 2 hard-cooked eggs, sliced
½ cup grated mozzarella cheese
    dash of grated Romano or
    Parmesan cheese**

1. Boil noodles according to directions on package and drain.

2. Preheat the oven to 350°.

3. In a square 8- by 8-inch baking dish or cake pan, layer ingredients in the following order: a small amount of sauce on the bottom; then noodles, meatballs, and egg slices; then another layer of sauce, topped with mozzarella cheese. (Save some sauce to pour over individual servings when ready to serve.)

4. Sprinkle with Romano or Parmesan cheese and bake for 20 minutes or until bubbling and hot through.

5. When done, remove Chinese Pasta from the oven and let cool slightly before cutting into squares for serving. Pour remaining sauce over each serving.

Serves 4 to 6

Spaghetti with meat sauce is a traditional Italian favorite that appeals to people of all ages.

Spaghetti with Meat Sauce/
Spaghetti al Sugo

Pasta is made fresh daily in Italy. In the north, it often takes the form of flat noodles. But around Naples, pasta is made in many shapes, from baby booties to little ears.

1 15-ounce can (about 2 cups) tomato sauce
1 12-ounce can (about 1½ cups) tomato paste
⅔ cup water
1 small onion, finely chopped
1 clove garlic, minced
1 3-ounce can mushroom pieces and liquid
½ teaspoon nutmeg
¼ cup sugar
1 pound lean ground beef
½ cup tomato juice or water
½ cup grated Parmesan cheese
8 ounces (½ pound) spaghetti noodles, uncooked
1 tablespoon vegetable oil

1. Combine tomato sauce, tomato paste, water, onion, garlic, mushrooms with liquid, nutmeg, and sugar in a Dutch oven.
2. Bring to a boil on top of the stove. Meanwhile, preheat the oven to 250°.
3. Cover and cook sauce in the oven for 2 hours. (Sauce can be cooked on top of the stove if simmered very slowly.)
4. After 2 hours, add ground beef. (You can crumble it into the sauce or shape it into meatballs about 1 inch in diameter.) Cook 1 hour.
5. Add tomato juice or water and cheese and cook for 20 minutes.
6. While sauce is cooking, prepare spaghetti *al dente,* following directions on package. (Be careful not to overcook spaghetti. Overcooked spaghetti will probably be too soft and will stick together. To keep spaghetti from becoming sticky during cooking, try putting 1 tablespoon vegetable oil in the water before boiling.)
7. Drain spaghetti and place on a deep platter. Cover with sauce and serve.

Serves 4 to 6

Italian-style pork chops is an elegant dish that is ideal to serve for a special occasion.

Italian-Style Pork Chops/
Costolette di Maiale Italiano

4 pork chops, about 1 inch thick
salt and pepper to taste
1 garlic clove, minced
1½ tablespoons olive or vegetable oil
½ cup canned tomato sauce
1 green pepper, cleaned out and cut
into thin strips
¼ pound fresh mushrooms, sliced, or
1 3-ounce can mushroom
pieces, drained
¾ teaspoon oregano
¼ cup tomato juice
4 ounces hot Italian sausage
(optional)

1. Trim excess fat from pork chops.
2. Mix salt, pepper, and garlic in a bowl. Rub on pork chops.
3. Heat oil in a large skillet and brown chops on both sides.
4. Add tomato sauce, green pepper, mushrooms, oregano, and tomato juice to the skillet. Stir. Cover and cook over low heat for about 30 minutes. (If you add sausage, brown it in a separate pan and drain. Add to the skillet during the last 10 minutes of cooking.)
5. Spoon sauce over chops and serve.

Serves 4

Be sure to use a large skillet when preparing Italian-style pork chops.

Chicken Hunter's Style/
Pollo alla Cacciatore

**a 2½- to 3-pound chicken, cut into
   serving pieces**
¼ cup butter
2 tablespoons olive or vegetable oil
1 cup finely chopped onion
**½ green pepper, cleaned out and
   chopped**
2 garlic cloves, minced
½ teaspoon basil
1 teaspoon salt
½ teaspoon pepper
1 cup stewed tomatoes, undrained
**½ cup tomato juice, canned chicken
   broth, or water**
**sliced mushrooms for garnish
   (optional)**

1. In a large skillet, brown chicken in
butter and oil over medium heat until
pieces are evenly brown on all sides.
2. Add onion, green pepper, garlic, basil,
salt, and pepper. Stir. Cook until onion is
soft but not brown (about 5 minutes).
3. Add undrained tomatoes and stir well.

Bring to a boil, cover, and cook over low
heat for 20 minutes, stirring occasionally.
4. Add tomato juice, chicken broth, or
water and simmer 10 minutes.
5. Remove chicken to serving dish and
spoon sauce over chicken. Garnish with
mushroom slices, if desired.

Serves 4

A sauce of tomatoes, green pepper, onion, and seasonings turns ordinary chicken into *pollo alla cacciatore.*

Bisignano Spinach/
Spinaci Bisignano

2 10-ounce packages frozen chopped spinach, cooked, or 1½ pounds fresh spinach, cooked and finely chopped
1 16-ounce carton (2 cups) ricotta or cottage cheese
1 cup bread crumbs or packaged herb stuffing
2 eggs, lightly beaten
¼ cup sliced fresh mushrooms or canned sliced mushrooms, drained
½ cup chopped green pepper
8 ounces (1 cup) sour cream
½ cup spaghetti sauce, canned or homemade (see page 31)
1 pound mozzarella cheese, sliced
1 teaspoon basil
½ cup grated Parmesan cheese

1. In a large bowl, combine spinach, ricotta or cottage cheese, bread crumbs, eggs, mushrooms, and green pepper.
2. Preheat the oven to 350°.
3. Pour mixture into a buttered 9- by 13-inch baking dish and spread sour cream on top.
4. Pour on a layer of spaghetti sauce, using most, but not all, of sauce. Cover with a layer of mozzarella cheese slices.
5. Spread remaining spaghetti sauce over cheese slices. Sprinkle with basil and Parmesan cheese.
6. Bake for 30 minutes.

Serves 6 to 8

Bisignano spinach and Italian-style cauliflower can be served as side dishes or as vegetarian main dishes.

Italian-Style Cauliflower/
Cavolfiore Italiano

1 head fresh cauliflower
4 tablespoons butter or margarine
1 small green pepper, cleaned out
**   and sliced**
¼ pound fresh mushrooms, sliced
2 tablespoons all-purpose flour
1 cup milk
1 pound mild pimento cheese, sliced

1. Cut core out of cauliflower and place its flower-shaped pieces in a large kettle of water. Bring water to a boil and cook cauliflower about 3 to 5 minutes. Drain.
2. Melt butter in a skillet and sauté pepper slices and mushrooms. (Add more butter if needed.)
3. Preheat the oven to 350°.
4. Remove the skillet from heat and sprinkle in flour a little at a time, stirring briskly.
5. Add milk slowly, stirring constantly. Return to heat and stir until mixture thickens.

6. Place cauliflower in a casserole dish. Lay cheese slices over cauliflower and pour creamed green pepper and mushrooms over the top. Bake 20 minutes.

Serves 6

SUPPER/
La Cena

An Italian supper is generally lighter than the midday meal, but it is just as delicious. It may consist of a nice thick soup, pizza, green salad, and fresh fruit for dessert. Since many parts of Italy have orchards and gardens, most families serve a wide variety of fresh fruits and vegetables daily.

If a family goes to a restaurant to eat supper, it is common to see little children with their heads down on the table, fast asleep. Since the Italians do not eat supper until about 8:00 P.M., the children sometimes have a hard time staying awake while the adults finish their meal.

Pizza makes a popular snack or light meal.

Pizza

The Italian pizzeria is a small shop with the counters lined with trays of pizza. Each tray features pizza slices with different toppings. The slices are just right for snacking as you stroll around town.

1 envelope active dry yeast
1 cup warm water
½ teaspoon salt
2 tablespoons olive or vegetable oil
2½ cups all-purpose flour
    pizza sauce (recipe follows)
8 ounces mozzarella cheese, grated
    (2 cups when grated)
    seasoned hamburger or other
    pizza toppings (recipe follows)

1. Dissolve yeast in 1 cup warm water. Stir in salt and oil. Gradually stir in flour. Beat vigorously 20 strokes. Let dough rest about 5 minutes.
2. Put dough in a warm place, cover with a damp towel, and let rise until double in size.
3. Punch dough down with your fist to let out the air. Divide dough in half.
4. Lightly grease 2 baking sheets or two 10-inch pizza pans. (If you prefer a thicker crust, use two 9-inch cake pans.) With floured fingers, pat each half of the dough into a 10-inch circle. (Dough should be thinly and evenly spread with no holes in it.) Build up edges of pizzas with your fingers. (This will keep sauce from running off.)
5. Spread pizza sauce over dough circles. Sprinkle with grated cheese and then with your favorite toppings.
6. Bake at 425° for 20 to 25 minutes. Let pizzas stand at least 5 minutes before cutting.

Makes 2 pizzas

No-Cook Pizza Sauce

1 6-ounce can (about ¾ cup) tomato
    paste
1 16-ounce can (2 cups) whole
    tomatoes, cut up with a spoon
2 cloves garlic, minced
1 teaspoon oregano
1 teaspoon basil
1 teaspoon olive or vegetable oil
¼ cup minced onion
1 green pepper, cleaned out and
    minced (optional)

1. In a large bowl, mix all ingredients
together with a fork.
2. Spoon sauce onto unbaked pizza crust.
Add topping, if desired, and bake as
directed in basic recipe on page 40.

Enough for 2 pizzas

Seasoned Hamburger Pizza Topping

*Seasoned hamburger is a topping that
everyone is sure to like. But it is also fun to
provide a variety of toppings for your
friends so that they can make their own
individual-style pizza. Good toppings to
try include mushrooms, green pepper,
sliced olives, pepperoni, salami, Italian
sausage, ham, and bacon.*

½ pound lean ground beef
⅛ to ¼ teaspoon salt
    pinch of pepper

1. Mix beef, salt, and pepper with a fork
or your fingers.
2. Drop beef in small chunks on top of
pizza sauce on unbaked pizza crust. Bake
as directed in basic recipe on page 40.

Enough for 2 pizzas

Biscuit tortoni is a sweet dessert that is very easy to prepare.

Biscuit Tortoni/
Tortoni

¾ **cup chilled whipping cream**
3 **tablespoons sugar**
½ **cup almond macaroon cookie
    crumbs**
1 **teaspoon almond extract**
2 **tablespoons chopped maraschino
    cherries**
¼ **cup chopped toasted almonds
    (optional)**

1. Line 6 muffin or custard cups with paper cupcake liners.
2. Beat whipping cream and sugar in a chilled bowl until stiff.
3. Set aside 2 tablespoons macaroon crumbs. Fold rest of crumbs, almond extract, cherries, and almonds into whipped cream.
4. Spoon mixture into prepared cups and sprinkle with remaining crumbs. Cover with aluminum foil or plastic wrap and freeze until firm (about 4 hours).

Serves 6

THE CAREFUL COOK

Whenever you cook, there are certain safety rules you must always keep in mind. Even experienced cooks follow these rules when they are in the kitchen.

1. Always wash your hands before handling food.

2. Thoroughly wash all raw vegetables and fruits to remove dirt, chemicals, and insecticides.

3. Use a cutting board when cutting up vegetables and fruits. Don't cut them up in your hand! And be sure to cut in a direction *away* from you and your fingers.

4. Long hair or loose clothing can easily catch fire if brought near the burners of a stove. If you have long hair, tie it back before you start cooking.

5. Turn all pot handles toward the back of the stove so that you will not catch your sleeve or jewelry on them. This is especially important when younger brothers and sisters are around. They could easily knock off a pot and get burned.

6. Always use a pot holder to steady hot pots or to take pans out of the oven. Don't use a wet cloth on a hot pan because the steam it produces could burn you.

7. Lift the lid of a steaming pot with the opening away from you so that you will not get burned.

8. If you get burned, hold the burn under cold running water. Do not put grease or butter on it. Cold water helps to take the heat out, but grease or butter will only keep it in.

9. If grease or cooking oil catches fire, throw baking soda or salt at the bottom of the flame to put it out. (Water will *not* put out a grease fire.) Call for help and try to turn all the stove burners to "off."

METRIC CONVERSION CHART

WHEN YOU KNOW	MULTIPLY BY	TO FIND
MASS (weight)		
ounces (oz)	28.0	grams (g)
pounds (lb)	0.45	kilograms (kg)
VOLUME		
teaspoons (tsp)	5.0	milliliters (ml)
tablespoons (Tbsp)	15.0	milliliters
fluid ounces (oz)	30.0	milliliters
cup (c)	0.24	liters (l)
pint (pt)	0.47	liters
quart (qt)	0.95	liters
gallon (gal)	3.8	liters
TEMPERATURE		
Fahrenheit (°F) temperature	5/9 (after subtracting 32)	Celsius (°C) temperature

COMMON MEASURES AND THEIR EQUIVALENTS

3 teaspoons = 1 tablespoon

8 tablespoons = ½ cup

2 cups = 1 pint

2 pints = 1 quart

4 quarts = 1 gallon

16 ounces = 1 pound

INDEX

ABOUT THE AUTHOR

Author **Alphonse "Babe" Bisignano** was born in Des Moines, Iowa, to an Italian family who originally came from the region of Calabria in southern Italy. Bisignano became a boxer at the age of 16, and at 18 he won the Iowa light-heavyweight championship. Then he went to New York and became a professional wrestler.

Bisignano returned to Iowa in 1939 and opened *Babe's Restaurant* in downtown Des Moines. The restaurant, which features Italian and American food, has been a popular Des Moines eating establishment ever since. Bisignano lives in Des Moines and is a member of the Iowa State Boxing Commission.

easy menu
ethnic
cookbooks